IS YOUR LIFE INSURANCE *OUTDATED?*

If your death benefit is only paid when you die, your life insurance is outdated.

George L. Stewart

Is Your Life Insurance Outdated?

ISBN 978-0-9993223-0-7

Printed in the United States of America

Dedication

This book is dedicated to all the caring life insurance agents who do their best to provide peace of mind and financial protection for their clients and their families.

It is also dedicated to all the individuals and families who own life insurance because they understand that someone would suffer financially if they were to die. They understand the importance and the value.

“Nothing is more powerful than an idea whose time has come.”

Victor Hugo

CONTENTS

Introduction

When I decided to write this book, I intended it to be a primer about a new, updated term life insurance that not only provides a death benefit, but also provides critical illness, chronic illness, and terminal illness coverage all in one policy, thereby creating "life insurance you don't have to die to collect."

Up until now, people buy traditional term life insurance for the possibility of collecting the death benefit. With this new updated term life insurance, "life insurance you don't have to die to collect," you can now own term life insurance with not just the possibility, but the probability of collecting the death benefit – and you don't have to die!

People now have a really valid reason to own term life insurance. It's not just for the peace of mind that comes with knowing their loved ones - or anyone else who might suffer financially by their death - are financially protected. But, more importantly, they now can effectively become their own beneficiary. They have a real probability of collecting the death benefit - not by dying, but by suffering a life threatening illness, thereby having a life threatening, medical crisis that is covered by the critical, chronic, or terminal illness benefits in the policy. A traditional term life insurance policy only pays when you die. Now you can own "life insurance you don't have to die to collect" that can pay up to 90% of the time, before you die.

As mentioned, I wanted this to be a primer - short, concise, and easy to read; informative and enlightening to the point that it would make people look at term life insurance in an entirely new and very different way. By effectively becoming their own beneficiary, folks now have not just a possibility, but a probability of collecting their death benefit - before they die.

“Life insurance you don’t have to die to collect” has a death benefit like a traditional term policy, but also includes a critical illness, chronic illness, and terminal illness benefit. What that means is, once you are stricken with a defined critical or chronic illness, or any terminal illness, you can collect the death benefit without dying. With the critical and chronic illness coverage, you don’t have to be terminally ill. In fact, many, if not most, who are stricken will recover and go on to lead a normal life. It’s not uncommon to be stricken with several life threatening illnesses, and recover, during one’s lifetime. With the terminal illness coverage, you can collect the death benefit up to 24 months before you are expected to die. Because of these additional benefits, you effectively become your own beneficiary.

Why is this important? Well, what happens before we die? We get sick! We are stricken with a life threatening illness; we suffer a medical crisis. Cancer, heart attack and stroke are considered the big three critical illnesses, accounting for over 80% of all deaths. By the time we reach the age of 65, 70% of us will have experienced at least one of these three illnesses. As mentioned, many, if not most of us will recover and go on to lead a long life. It’s not uncommon to have a second, or more, critical or chronic illness. Any one of these might be the eventual cause of death.

Life expectancy is now about 80 years of age. “Life insurance you don’t have to die to collect,” is available to age 90. What this means is, statistics indicate, you would have over a 90% probability of being able to collect the death benefit before you reach age 90 without dying. That’s because the probability is up to 90%, and more, that you will be stricken with a life threatening illness at least once and experience a defined medical crisis before age 90.

This multi-benefit policy makes any traditional term life insurance policy - one that only pays the death benefit when the insured dies - outdated.

The question is: would you rather own a traditional term life insurance policy that has a very small possibility of paying the death benefit – and you have to die for it to pay - or would you rather own this new, updated term life insurance that also includes critical, chronic, and terminal illness benefits that offer up to a 90% probability of paying – and you don't have to die to collect?

The answer is: own "life insurance you don't have to die to collect."

Chapter 1

Why I'm writing this book.

Someone told me that if you can't find any information about a specific topic because there is no book, and there is not much information available, you probably should be the one to write that book.

Life insurance is one of those topics that most people would rather not talk about. It falls under the conversation group that might include; shopping for a car, visiting the I.R.S., having a procedure such as a root canal, and other sundry subjects.

To paraphrase one of the TV commercials, "people tend to buy life insurance and forget about it." Not only do most people forget about it, they really don't want to talk about it, even after they have purchased it.

I'm going to introduce you to an entirely new and different way to own term life insurance. By the end of my book, I hope that you will understand that there is a new reason and a new way to own term life insurance. This new product enables the insured person to collect the death benefit before they die. They effectively become their own beneficiary. That's something worth talking about.

Life insurance is typically purchased for peace of mind; a specific purpose. Those who own life insurance seldom expect to use it. Few people think they are going to die. They know they will eventually, but they don't expect to, at least not for a while. For the most part, their thinking is correct. The truth is, very few term life insurance policies are ever paid. More about that later.

So, here we go. I'm going to show you a type of life insurance that most people have never heard of. In fact, many, if not most, life insurance agents aren't familiar with it. There are only a handful of insurance companies that offer it and they don't advertise it.

We all know we're going to die. That's a 100% certainty. That's why we buy life insurance; to protect the ones we care about; the ones who would be hurt financially when we die. But, what happens before we die? We get sick. How many people do you think die healthy? Virtually none.

Traditional term life insurance is very basic. You buy a policy, you pay a premium, you die, the company pays the death benefit to your beneficiary. End of you. End of story.

But, wait. What if you could collect the death benefit when you are stricken with a life threatening illness and experience a medical crisis? You wouldn't have to wait until you die so the insurance company could pay someone else your death benefit. You could be your own beneficiary. You could collect your own death benefit. How good would that be?

I'm going to introduce you to "life insurance you don't have to die to collect," a combination of traditional term life insurance and supplemental insurance that includes critical illness, chronic illness, and terminal illness coverage.

Consider this to be your insurance primer about a new, different, and updated way to own life insurance.

Chapter 2

What is life insurance?

Life insurance is a contract, commonly referred to as a policy, between the insured person and the insurance company.

All life insurance policies have three primary parties; the insured, the policy owner, and the beneficiary(s). These three parties are all required when applying for life insurance.

In all traditional life insurance policies, the insured is the person whose life is being protected. In other words, the covered individual is the insured person. The death benefit is paid when their death occurs. The life insurance premiums are based primarily upon the insured's age, gender, overall health, amount of the death benefit, occupation, and other qualifying factors at the time of the application. Please note: It is easier to qualify for a $100,000 death benefit than it is for a $1,000,000 death benefit.

Besides the insured person, there is an owner of the policy, sometimes referred to as the policy holder or simply policy owner. Typically, the owner is also the insured person; however, that is not always the case. Sometimes it can be someone else such as the spouse, a business partner, or anyone who has an insurable interest. The owner is responsible for paying the premiums and making sure the policy doesn't lapse. The owner also has the right to make changes to the policy. While the owner can't change the name of the insured, he can change everything else such as the beneficiary, and the payment information, e.g. bank information or mode of payment such as monthly, quarterly, semi-annually, or annually. The owner is the only one authorized to discuss the insurance policy with the insurance company.

Finally, there is the beneficiary. The beneficiary is the person(s) who receives the proceeds, or death benefit, of the policy when the insured person dies. The beneficiary could be the spouse, the family, business partners, someone the insured is supporting such as elderly parents, or anyone else who has an insurable interest.

There can be more than one beneficiary. The beneficiaries are usually listed in a specific order: primary, contingent and tertiary. If the primary beneficiary dies before the insured, the contingent beneficiary receives the proceeds. Sometimes there is a reason to name a third, or tertiary, beneficiary. There can also be co-beneficiaries such as two or more children who would share in the proceeds.

There are basically two types of life insurance, permanent and term.

Permanent life insurance means the insurance is typically lifelong and there is some type of cash accumulation. You may pay premiums up to age 121, or less, as defined by the policy. The death benefit exists as long as the premiums are paid. There are numerous types of permanent life insurance. Two popular examples of permanent life insurance are whole life and universal life.

Term life insurance means the premium is only paid for the term designated by the policy, typically anywhere from 1 year to 35 years. You pay premiums for the term duration or until you die, whichever comes first. The payments, or premiums, for term policies are considerably cheaper than permanent policies because there is no cash accumulation and there is a very low payout by the insurance companies. That's mainly because the policies are usually written for a short term and at an age when deaths are least likely to occur.

Term life insurance is the basis for this book. All references, examples, and comparisons refer to term policies only, unless otherwise noted. All of the premium examples are based on a male, non-smoker, in excellent health, and are the best rates available.

Chapter Three

What is traditional term life insurance and why is it considered outdated?

Traditional term life insurance is simply life insurance that pays a benefit in the event of the death of the insured during a specified time period or term.

Traditional term life insurance can now be considered outdated for two reasons:

The product itself.
The death benefit is only paid when there is a death. The insured has to die and only then is the death benefit paid to a beneficiary.

Conventional wisdom.
Conventional wisdom is that people need term insurance for a specific purpose; a time period in their life when there is a risk of financial hardship; such as making sure the mortgage is paid off; the kids get out of college; that there's money for the family if the insured passes away during this time. This is great for peace of mind. Most often, however, the term period is for a period when there is a possibility the insured person might die, not when there is a probability they might die.

The new, updated term life insurance not only includes a death benefit, but also includes three additional benefits: critical, chronic, and terminal illness coverage. Since the probability is that the insured person most likely will suffer a medical crisis or two, or even more, before actually dying, it makes sense to have the ability to collect the death benefit when this occurs, and without dying.

The risk of dying during most life insurance term periods is actually very low because life expectancy is currently around 80 years old. The younger you are when you buy life insurance, the less likely you are to die. The insured person typically outlives a traditional term life insurance policy. It just expires because the term is up. People are seldom shown the numerous ways and reasons to buy term life insurance. You should consider owning life insurance until you're at least 80 because the younger you are, the less chance you have that the death benefit will be paid. The outdated traditional term life insurance death benefit is actually paid only a very small portion of the time

Let's consider a 40-year-old male who's a husband, a father, and has two kids in school. He buys a $500,000 term policy for 20 years. His monthly premium is approximately $35.00 (yes, it can be that cheap.) His total premium cost for twenty years is $8,400 or $420 per year. What happens in 20 years when he turns 60? The house will be paid off, the kids will be out of college and he no longer has a need for the $500,000 term policy. He also no longer has any life insurance because it expired. But, what happened during the 20 years that he paid on this term policy for $500,000. He protected his family for the mortgage, the kids going to college, and had peace of mind for those twenty years.

But, he really only had a small chance of dying. Now consider this. Owning traditional term life insurance until age 80 is not expensive. That $500,000 term policy for 40 years from age 40 to 80 is about $31,200 in total premiums. That's spread out over the forty years and averages less than $800 per year. If he has traditional term life insurance to age 80, he has over a 50% chance of collecting the death benefit. When he bought it to age 60 he had only a very small chance of collecting. Instead of buying any term life insurance to a certain age, say 60, - which is an age that your probability of dying is not that great - instead, continue that term policy to age 80. That would increase your probability of collecting the death benefit to over 50%. If you owned “life insurance you don’t have to die to collect,” your probability of collecting the death benefit increases to over 80% and you don’t have to die! In reality, you have over a 70 % chance of collecting the death benefit by age 65, and you don’t have to die. That’s because at age 65 over 70% of men and women will have been stricken with a life threatening disease - specifically cancer, stroke or heart disease) - and suffered a medical crisis. By the way, those three illnesses are considered the big three critical illnesses and account for over 80% of all deaths.

If you’re going to spend money on premiums, why not take advantage of an opportunity to actually be able to collect your death benefit before you die. Owning life insurance and paying premiums to an older age is not gambling when you’ll die. You’re simply confronting the inevitable.

This book is written not only to inform the uninsured, but also to enlighten the people who already own life insurance. These folks recognize the value and the need for it. They also understand how inexpensive it is. Traditional term life insurance is outdated because the only way the death benefit is paid is when the insured dies. Of course, the insured person doesn’t get the money. It is paid to their beneficiary.

Traditional term life insurance also outdated because the term period for the coverage is for a period when there is a possibility the insured person might die, not when there is a probability they might die.

Most importantly, your probability of being stricken with any critical, chronic, or terminal illness is greater than dying at any age.

Chapter 4

What is supplemental insurance?

Supplemental insurance can refer to a broad range of insurance products and coverage.

A Medicare Supplement is insurance commonly referred to as a Medigap policy and sold by private companies. It can help pay some of the health care costs that original medicare doesn't cover, such as co-payments, co-insurance, and deductibles.

Another type of supplemental insurance is extra, or additional, medical insurance that you can purchase to help pay for services and out-of-pocket expenses that your regular, non-Medicare, insurance does not cover. These supplemental insurance plans will also pay for out-of-pocket medical expenses, such as, co-payments, co-insurance, and deductibles.

Other supplemental insurance will pay cash benefits when you're sick or hurt to help with expenses not covered by your medical insurance. These include short term disability coverage, hospital insurance, and dental coverage, just to name a few. There are a wide variety of supplemental insurance plans available.

Another type of supplemental coverage is critical illness coverage such as cancer policies. These stand alone policies have been around for a while. They pay a lump sum to the insured when the insured is diagnosed with cancer as defined in the policy. These policies eventually evolved to include heart attack and stroke. They are defined as critical illness policies and may offer additional coverage as defined in the policy. There is no life insurance, or death benefit, included.

A typical supplemental insurance policy that could include coverage for cancer, heart attack and stroke may look something like this: the issue age could start at 18 and continue through age 89, although some companies will not let you purchase it after age 75. Many companies will limit you to a maximum of $100,000. The rates typically increase every 5 years. A cost example could look something like this. A 50 year old individual would spend about $85 a month for a $50,000 benefit. By age 80 it would be up to almost $180.00 a month.

While the probability is 70% that by age 65 you would collect this benefit, there is a cheaper way to obtain not only similar coverage but, chronic illness, terminal illness, and additional defined critical illness coverage, plus a life insurance benefit. As a cost example, a $100,000 "life insurance you don't have to die to collect" policy that includes critical, chronic, and terminal illness benefits, would be about $42 per month for a 50 year old through age 80. That also includes a life insurance benefit of $100,000. The result is more substantial coverage for much less premium. Also, the premium will remain the same for the term.

These additional critical, chronic, and terminal illness benefits are sometimes referred to as "living benefits." These benefits are especially important because your probability of being stricken with any critical, chronic, or terminal illness is greater than dying at any age.

Chapter 5

What is "life insurance you don't have to die to collect?"

I always enjoy seeing people's reaction when I tell them I've written a book. When I say it's about life insurance their eyes usually roll and their curiosity wanes. It's humorous to see some of the responses.

So, I'm writing about something that is really exciting – life insurance! ……Wait. You don't think life insurance is exciting? That's okay. Neither did I until I discovered this amazing product that you're going to learn about over the next chapters. Most people have never heard of it and not many life insurance agents are familiar with it. It's called "life insurance you don't have to die to collect."

We all know that life insurance is purchased to reduce or eliminate financial suffering when someone dies. Traditionally, you buy a policy; you have a death benefit; you pay the premium; you die. The death benefit is then paid to the beneficiary. The important thing to remember here is that the death benefit is paid then, and only then, when the insured dies. It doesn't matter what type of life insurance you have or the reason you have it. It could be term life, whole life, universal life or any other type of life insurance. The point is, the death benefit is only paid when the death of the insured person occurs and it's then paid to the beneficiary. As mentioned, the beneficiary could be the spouse, children, other family members, business partners, someone you're supporting like elderly parents, or anyone else who might suffer financially because of the death of the insured. That pretty much describes traditional term life insurance.

We all know we're going to die. That's a 100% certainty. The reality is that almost all of us will suffer at least one, and sometimes two or more, medical crises before we die.

Sudden deaths are rare. Less than 8% of all deaths are due to unnatural causes; accident, suicide, and homicide. So that means that over 92% of us will die of natural causes – we'll get sick first – and have at least one medical crisis before we die.

What is a medical crisis? A medical crisis occurs when someone is stricken with a life threatening illness. A life threatening illness is any illness that will result in death without treatment. Three examples of a medical crisis are – cancer, heart attack, and stroke. There are other types of medical crises, but these are the top three, accounting for over 80% of all deaths.

What typically follows a medical crisis? Financial suffering or, at worst, a financial crisis.

Examples of a financial crisis are: loss of income and the inability to cover normal living expenses. New medical expenses can be high deductibles, medication not covered, experimental treatment not covered, transportation costs for out of area medical visits, lifestyle changes, such as home remodeling for wheelchair access. .... and the list goes on. There can be many related and unforeseen expenses when a medical crisis occurs.

Let's look at some statistics. Heart attacks, strokes, and cancer account for over 80% of all deaths. More than one in three of us will be diagnosed with heart disease. Every 40 seconds someone has a stroke. One in two men and one in three women will be stricken with some type of cancer in their lifetime. It is estimated that there are over 5,000 new cases of cancer diagnosed every day.

70% of all of us who reach the age of 65 will have been stricken with cancer, heart attack, or stroke and survived. That's 7 out of 10 people who reach the age of 65. More amazing is the fact that the average of the first incident of cancer, heart attack, or stroke is 43. That's the average age!

What do you think will happen first, a medical crisis or a death crisis? Are you going to get sick first or are you going to die first? I think we all know the answer to that. Virtually no one dies healthy.

I think we all understand how our lives will play out before we actually die. Many, if not most of us will have at least one medical crisis before we die and that will probably be followed by a financial crisis, or at the very least, financial suffering, – all of this before we die,

The good news is that many, if not most, people who are stricken with a life threatening illness and suffer a medical crisis, will survive and go on to live a long time. In fact, it's not uncommon for someone to have more than one medical crisis and still live a long time.

Okay, so far, this hasn't been very exciting. But, we have to look at the realistic part before we can look at the exciting part.

So, here's the exciting part.

Think about this. What if, when you have a medical crisis and it's followed by a financial crisis - meaning you need money – what if, you, the insured, could collect the death benefit of your life insurance policy? That's the money that's just sitting there, waiting for you to die. How exciting would that be?

"Life insurance you don't have to die to collect" will allow you to collect the death benefit if you need the cash because of a medical crisis. You now effectively become your own beneficiary.

This ability to collect the death benefit is an option, You don't have to collect it. You aren't required to collect it. But, the choice is there if you need, or want, the money. Yes, you can now collect the death benefit when you have a medical crisis and don't die.

It works like this. Once you are diagnosed by your doctor with a critical, chronic, or terminal illness, as defined by the insurance company, they will determine, with your doctor, the severity of your illness. The maximum settlement is typically 65% to 85% of the death benefit. They will not let you collect 100% of the death benefit. They limit the maximum benefit to approximately 85%. They can pay less than 85% because not all illnesses are the same severity.

Let's say you have a $500,000 death benefit and are stricken with cancer. The insurance company determines that it's a severe case and the settlement option is 75%. That means you can collect 75% of $500,000 as a cash settlement if you so choose. 75% of $500,000 is $375,000. The insurance company will write a check for $375,000, made out to you, to spend as you see fit. You can use the money for any purpose you choose. You could use it for lost income, medical expenses, experimental treatment, living expenses, pay off your house, even take the family on a vacation. You do not have to account for how the money will be spent or provide any receipts. The policy is ended. There are no more premiums. You can collect a portion and still have a reduced death benefit. In that case, the monthly premium would be reduced appropriately to match the new death benefit. If you take the full settlement of $375,000, the policy is ended. There is no more death benefit or premium.

Here's how the option works. Just because the insured qualifies to collect the death benefit, he doesn't have to collect all of it, part of it, or any of it. If he doesn't need the money, he has the choice to forgo collecting the death benefit early. He can wait until he dies and the money is paid to his beneficiary, or he can wait until he has another medical crisis and opt to collect the death benefit at that time. The worst that could happen is this: he doesn't collect the benefit the first time it's available; He doesn't suffer another qualifying medical crisis. He lives to a ripe old age and the term insurance expires before he does. He now gets nothing. Remember that this is a term policy and expires at a certain age, one that the insured may choose to own to age 90. When he suffered a qualifying illness that gave him the opportunity to collect the death benefit early, that might have been his only bite of the apple or his only ability to collect the death benefit. If he recovers, as many who are stricken do, he may not have another qualifying illness, or even die, before the term is up.

Finally, and most importantly, you don't have to be terminally ill. Many who are stricken will survive and live long lives. Besides insuring your life if you die, you're actually insuring you best asset – your ability to sustain your quality of life – and you can have money when you may need it most.

The cost for "life insurance you don't have to die to collect," that pays when you have a medical crisis, is about the same, and sometimes less, than outdated traditional life insurance that only pays when you die.

Now that's exciting!

benefit early. He can wait until he dies and the money is paid to his beneficiary, or he can wait until he has [illegible] and [illegible] to collect the [illegible] benefit [illegible]. The worst thing that happens is that he doesn't get the benefit [illegible] while he's still alive. He doesn't [illegible] a [illegible] medical [illegible] [illegible] [illegible] [illegible] [illegible] [illegible] [illegible]

[illegible]

[illegible] which are [illegible] will [illegible] [illegible] [illegible] [illegible] you [illegible] quality of life [illegible] when you may need it most.

[illegible]

[illegible]

Chapter 6

What are "living benefits?"

The primary benefit, and usually the only benefit, with traditional term life insurance policies is a death benefit. The death benefit is only paid when the insured person dies. "Life insurance you don't have to die to collect" is made up of a death benefit and three living benefits.

A living benefit is a benefit that can be collected without the insured person's dying. The three types of living benefits are: critical illness, chronic illness, and terminal illness coverage. "Life insurance you don't have to die to collect" includes the death benefit and all of the aforementioned living benefits.

While we all know we are going to die, we must recognize a more important fact. Almost all of us will be stricken with a life threatening illness before we die. We need to be aware that getting sick and suffering a defined medical crisis can enable the insured to collect the death benefit without dying. Suffering a medical crisis doesn't mean we are going to die. It just means we have been stricken with a critical or chronic illness. Most will recover and live a long time. In fact, many will be stricken and recover multiple times in their lifetime. These medical crises may present the option of collecting the death benefit without dying.

The critical illness living benefit has been available as a stand alone policy for some time. It was originally available only as a supplemental cancer policy. It would pay a pre-determined benefit if the policy holder were stricken with cancer as defined in the policy. These policies eventually evolved to include heart attack and stroke. There is no life insurance, or death benefit, included with these stand alone policies. As of this writing, the critical illness living benefit with "life insurance you don't have to die to collect" can include up to seventeen defined critical illnesses, depending on the life insurance company.

The chronic illness living benefit is relatively new and unique because of it's defined coverage. If the insured is unable to perform any two of the six activities of daily living, they would be eligible to collect the death benefit. It may also include severe cognitive impairment such as Alzheimer's Disease and forms of similar irreversible dementia, as defined by the insurance company.

The terminal illness living benefit has been around for years as simply a terminal illness rider. Only recently has it been referred to as a living benefit. The insured can collect the death benefit if he is diagnosed with a terminal illness with a life expectancy of 12 to 24 months, depending on the policy guidelines.

"Life insurance you don't have to die to collect" that includes the three living benefits, now gives you four ways to collect your death benefit. You can collect when one of the four benefits, death, critical illness, chronic illness, or terminal illness, occurs.

It should be noted that no part of living benefits is any kind of long term care, health care benefits, or any kind of disability coverage.

Because of living benefits, there are now several reasons to own this new, updated term life insurance. Own it for the death benefit. The supplemental benefits are a bonus. If you have excellent medical benefits or just don't think you would have a financial crisis when you have a medical crisis, then own it first for the death benefit. But, if you are healthy and suddenly suffer a medical crisis, you might want the option of collecting the living benefit, especially if you're near the end of the term. In other words, if the insurance is going to expire soon, you may not collect anything if you don't opt to collect the living benefit.

Many folks don't have any health insurance, or what they have is limited. This new, updated term life insurance is ideal because you can collect the death benefit when you are stricken with a defined illness. Now you have cash to use for whatever your needs may be. It could be for the deductibles, treatments that aren't paid for, costly prescriptions, lost income, whatever. You don't have to collect the entire death benefit to use when you are stricken with a critical, chronic, or even terminal illness. You can collect a partial amount and leave the balance as a death benefit. Please note that this is an alternative, not a substitute, for health insurance

Few of us want to consider our end of life and the events that lead up to, and follow, it. But, traditional term life insurance allows us peace of mind when confronting the inevitable. The best part about "life insurance you don't have to die to collect" is that your probability of being stricken with any critical, chronic, or terminal illness is much greater than dying at any age. Better that you collect your death benefit before you die, rather than it be collected by someone else after you die – or not collected at all because the term expired before you did.

It's important to note here that the maximum living benefit coverage available is up to $2,000,000 as defined in the policy. If the death benefit is over $2,000,000, the maximum amount that could be collected is based on $2,000,000, not the higher death benefit. If the insured had a higher death benefit, for example, $3,000,000 and wanted to collect the maximum amount, he could only collect up to $2,000,000. The difference would remain as a death benefit, with an adjusted, reduced premium.

That all being said, would you rather own a traditional term life insurance policy that pays only a small portion of the time; or would you rather own "life insurance you don't have to die to collect" that can pay up to 90% of the time ...and you don't have to die?

Now, that's really exciting!

Chapter 7

What is a medical crisis?

A medical crisis, in the context here, occurs when the insured is stricken with a life threatening illness; a critical, chronic, or terminal illness as defined in the policy.

To reiterate, "life insurance you don't have to die to collect" is made up of traditional term life insurance coverage that includes not only the death benefit, but also includes critical illness, chronic illness, and terminal illness coverage so that you now have the best of both worlds. It will pay when you die, but more importantly it will pay when you are stricken with a life threatening illness and suffer a medical crisis as defined by one of the three additional benefits. This is what will happen to over 80% of policy holders who have coverage to age 80. They now have over an 80% probability of collecting the death benefit before they die.

This exciting, updated term life insurance includes the three additional benefits as no-cost riders. Life insurance riders are addon provisions that provide additional benefits to a primary policy. They come into play when a specific condition is met.

Let's define these three different kinds of illness coverages.

1. *A critical illness* is classified as a life threatening condition caused by one of the specific critical illness listed.

Depending on the insurance company, critical illness coverage, by definition, is any one of the following individual illnesses. No one company covers all the critical illnesses listed, just most of them.

1. Heart attack or coronary artery bypass
2. Invasive Cancer
3. Stroke
4. End stage renal failure
5. Major organ transplant
6. ALS (Amyotrophic Lateral Sclerosis)
7. Blindness
8. Paralysis
9. Coma
10. Major burns
11. Arterial aneurysms
12. Central nervous system tumors
13. Major multi-system trauma
14. Auto-immune deficiency syndrome (AIDS)
15. Severe disease of any organ
16. Severe central nervous system disease
17. Loss of limbs

Until now, critical illness policies were stand alone policies. That means you could purchase a critical illness policy that typically only covered heart attack, cancer and stroke. The amount of coverage was limited, it was not inexpensive, and the rates typically increased every 5 years. It usually would end at age 75. There was no life insurance; that is, no death benefit was included. These policies are considered to be supplemental insurance and are still available to purchase. They initially were offered as cancer policies and only covered cancer. These policies now include coverage for heart attacks and stroke, in addition to cancer.

2. A chronic illness is one that lasts at least three months and may or may not be the result of a critical illness. In the context here, a chronic illness is any illness or condition in which the insured is unable to perform at least two of the six activities of daily living.

The activities of daily living are:
Bathing
Continence
Dressing
Eating
Toileting
Transferring

It may also include severe cognitive impairment such as Alzheimer's Disease and forms of similar irreversible dementia.

This is important coverage because, as an example, it could cover someone who is injured in an accident and subsequently confined to a wheelchair. Because they are confined to a wheelchair and typically could not perform two of the six daily activities of living, they would qualify for collecting the death benefit under the chronic illness coverage benefit. By definition, chronic illness coverage is another way the insured can qualify to collect the death benefit.

3. A terminal illness is any illness or chronic condition that is reasonably expected to result in the insured's death within twelve to twenty four months. The term is determined by each life insurance company and may vary.

It's important to reiterate that your probability of being stricken with any critical, chronic, or terminal illness is greater than dying at any age.

As mentioned, "Life insurance you don't have to die to collect" now gives you the opportunity to collect your death benefit before you die. The probability is now over 80% that this will occur by age 80. It increases to 90% by age 90.

If you own “life insurance you don’t have to die to collect” with a one year, ten year, twenty year, or a thirty five year term (or anything in between), the premium stays the same for the entire period. The best part is that the premium for this new policy that includes critical illness, chronic illness and terminal illness coverage, is about the same as the cost for comparable, traditional life insurance policies that only pay when you die. Sometimes the cost is even less.

Chapter 8

The kids get the money but who gets the kids?

As I got into writing the different chapters, I realized that providing for the family financially - the spouse and children - may be paramount, but, what would happen to the kids if both parents died or became incapacitated? The kids would now have the life insurance money, but who would handle the money, take care of them, and raise them. I knew I had to include this chapter. It doesn't matter how protected the family is financially, how else do you protect the kids?

Most parents will tell you that their most precious asset is their children. Yet many of these are the same folks who have no provision for the kids if both parents were to die or become incapacitated. Too many parents don't have a clue, much less a plan, on how to protect their children's future if they were to die or become incapacitated. These same parents sometimes don't have life insurance because they don't recognize the value or need. If the parents have a sizable estate and can provide for their children financially should both die, or become incapacitated, they may not need life insurance. But, remember that life insurance is for anyone who might suffer financially if someone were to die. Not many would suffer more than minor children.

This topic is one of those life subjects that fall under the category, "I don't know the answers." That's because sometimes not only do we not know the answers, we don't even know the questions. Read on and allow me to give you some direction.

Generally speaking, in most states, if there is no legal guardian designated, any child under the age of 18 becomes a ward of the state as a protected person. They would then be placed with the closest relative or in foster care with an appointed guardian until an official guardian is appointed by the state. That process can take up to two years - and sometimes longer.

What that means is, if you don't legally designate who should take care of your children, the state will decide. Just verbally telling, or asking, someone to take care of your children if something happens is not good enough. The court is the ultimate decider.

In many states, only a traditional will, or a pour over will in a trust, can be used to designate a child's personal guardian. In other states it can be done with a special affidavit. Typically, no other type of document, including a living trust by itself, will work. The guardian can also be referred to as the conservator. In some states the conservator is the one who handles the minor's finances and can be a separate person. The personal guardian that is appointed by the will or affidavit only becomes the legal guardian after approval by the court. The judge does have the authority to name someone else if he is convinced that it is in the best interest of the child to do so. This could happen if the nominee has obvious problems, such as alcoholism, a criminal background, child abuse history, or if objections have been filed. An alternate personal guardian should always be selected in case the first cannot serve, or refuses to serve. If there is a separate conservator, an alternate should also be named.

One of the first things that should be done is designate someone who would take charge immediately if both parents were to die or become incapacitated. For example, if both parents were killed or incapacitated, and the kids were with a babysitter, would the sitter know whom to call? When the authorities come to the house, if the sitter has no one to whom to refer them, the children may go to Child Protective Services and be placed in foster care. You should have someone who can be immediately available and can also show they have the authority to take custody of your children, at least temporarily. Next you need to designate someone to take care of the children permanently if both parents were to die or become incapacitated. It is not enough to name someone, be it family members or friends, and verbally agree that they will take custody of your children should that need arise. Any decision you make, any conclusion you reach, needs to be in a legally binding, written contract. The state still will ultimately determine who the legal guardian will be, but they will abide by your wishes unless the judge determines the named guardian(s) may not be in the best interest of the children. You should always have an alternate guardian (and conservator if necessary) in case the first named can't, or chooses not to, participate. If you are having difficulty choosing a guardian, you are still better off choosing someone sooner rather than later. If something happens before you decide, then the court will decide for you. In many cases the court's plan may not be the one you would have wanted. It's not uncommon to have children being raised by someone the parents would not have chosen to do so. Make a decision before it's too late. You can always change it later. Time really is of the essence.

Once you've mutually decided who the legal guardian will be, the next thing is to discuss how you want your children raised. This should actually be a major consideration when choosing a guardian. You want to be sure everyone is on the same page.

Next, you want to be sure there are assets to provide resources for someone to raise the kids. It doesn't matter if you have little assets or a lot, the guardian needs to have access. Whether you have a sizable amount of cash from your estate, a life insurance death benefit or whatever, one of the major decisions is how that money is dispersed to the children. For example, should the guardians have access to the money all at once or should there be a monthly payment. This is only one of many decisions you will have to prepare for.

For many, writing a will is more about naming guardians for the children than it is about distributing assets. Let me repeat that. For many, writing a will is more about naming guardians for the children than it is about distributing assets. If you have any assets at all, you may want to consider a living trust instead of a will. This will eliminate the estate going through probate. Probate takes time, can be costly, and is public. A living trust is much quicker, there is little cost, and your estate is kept private. If you are not familiar with the difference between a will and a living trust, do some research online if you can and then see an attorney. Many attorneys will initially consult with you for free. You need to know the differences between a will and a living trust, and how it applies to you.

If you have a sizable estate and there is money that the children will eventually receive, there are trusts that can be set up for them so there is control as to how the money is dispersed. Again, consult with an attorney familiar with estate planning.

I could write pages offering scenarios, giving advice, and just plain opining, but I just wanted to touch the surface of what can happen to the kids when both parents die or become incapacitated.

These are topics that should be handled by an attorney who specializes in, or is familiar with, estate planning and guardianship. Laws vary from state to state. Select one that is convenient to you and licensed in your state. Remember, you don't have to use the first one you talk to. Don't be afraid to speak to several until you find one you're most comfortable with.

My final advice: see an attorney as soon as possible.

Chapter 9

Once upon a time - the story of Bob and Jim.

This is the story of Bob and Jim, two lifelong friends, who are the same age. They grew up on the same block. They went to the same schools and graduated from the same college. They married their high school sweethearts, had children, worked at similar jobs at different companies, and pretty much led parallel lives.

At age 45, Bob and Jim each bought a $500,000 term life insurance policy. Both policies were for 35 years, or until both would be age 80. At age 60 each was stricken with a life threatening critical illness that would keep them from working for 12 months. The good news is, they both survived and went on to live long lives.

What's important to consider here is the journey they each took from the time they were stricken until the time they recovered. First, there were many unforeseen expenses such as many medical bills, experimental treatment costs, and high deductibles that had to be paid. Their medical coverage only paid a portion of the medical expenses. There was also lost income. Normal living expenses still had to be covered. The cost of each of their illnesses was about $150,000 over that 12 month period. Bob had little savings other than his 401k. He took as much out of it as he could. His wife had to go back to work. At some point they got behind on their house payment and had to move into an apartment. Bob eventually recovered and went back to work but the medical crisis was financially devastating. His family's quality of life never recovered. Bob was able keep up the payments on his traditional term life insurance policy, so he was still covered til age 80.

Jim, on the other hand, didn't own a traditional term life insurance policy like Bob. He owned "life insurance you don't have to die to collect." Like Bob's policy, Jim's has a death benefit. But, it also had three additional benefits called living benefits. It included critical illness coverage that would allow him to collect the death benefit if he were stricken with a defined critical illness such as cancer, heart attack, or stroke. When Jim got sick, he was off work for twelve months like Bob, and suffered the same $150,000 in expenses and lost income. However, he was able to collect the death benefit of his policy because he was his own beneficiary. He decided to collect the maximum amount available. Jim was able to collect 70% of the death benefit or $350,000. (remember, the amount collected will never be 100% of the death benefit. It will be adjusted according to the severity of the illness and the terms of the policy.) Having opted to collect the maximum amount, his policy is ended. There is no remaining death benefit and nothing to pay back. It is a final settlement.

The insurance company wrote a check - made out to Jim - to use any way he chose. After covering the $150,000 in expenses, he had $200,000 in cash. He can do whatever he wants to with the money. For example, he can take the $200,000, purchase an annuity, or some other guaranteed cash accumulation vehicle, and double his money in ten years. So in 10 years, at age 70, he could have $400,000.

Since Bob and Jim both recovered and lived well into their eighties, Bob never benefited from his term policy because it expired when he turned 80.

As a comparison, Bob's $500,000 traditional term life insurance policy cost $106 a month for 35 years. ($106 X 12 months X 35 years). That's a total of $44,520 for traditional peace of mind. Jim's policy cost $110 per month, also for 35 years. But, because he was able to collect the death benefit after 15 years, his total premiums paid was only $19,800. When he did that, the policy was terminated. He had no coverage and no premiums due, just the $350,000 in cash.

Summing this up, we see that Bob got $500,000 of life insurance for 35 years and it only cost him $44,520. Had he died, it would have been a great return on the money spent. Jim, however, only paid for his term life insurance policy for 15 years because he was able to collect the death benefit early when he suffered a critical illness. He was able to collect $350,000 for $19,800 paid in premiums. After he covered the $150,000 in expenses, he had $200,000 in cash that he could use anyway he chose.

Bob purchased his traditional term life insurance based on the possibility of dying before the term was up. Jim purchased his new, updated term life insurance based on the probability of suffering a medical crisis before the term was up and he wouldn't have to die to collect the death benefit.

Traditional term life insurance is perfect for what it's designed to do. It covers a person for a period of time, for a specific reason, and provides peace of mind.

On the other hand, "life insurance you don't have to die to collect" or term life insurance with three additional benefits called "living benefits," now gives customers a new perspective on life insurance. The approach now is that they should be covered at least until they're 80. That would give them over an 80% chance of collecting the death benefit before they die simply based on the probability that they will be stricken with a critical, chronic, or terminal illness - before they die.

It's not a question of if you'll be stricken before you die. The question is when.

Chapter 10

Life insurance is actually inexpensive. How do they do that?

Most of us have seen the ads on television or heard them on the radio. "Joe Smith, 40 years old, just bought a $250,000 life insurance policy for less than $17.00 a month. Now, he feels good knowing his family is protected." The announcer then says that Joe is healthy and the policy is a ten year term policy.

Here's the reality. That is the actual cost, and it is that cheap. So how do the insurance companies do that?
The monthly premium quoted is because Joe is a non-smoker, he's in good health, he's young, and it's a short, term policy. The chances of Joe dying before the term is up are very slim. He's more likely to stop making the premiums for some reason than he is to actually die.

He may let the policy lapse for any number of reasons. He may have gotten a new job that provides him with life insurance. He may have suffered a loss of income because of a job change. Something may have happened that created more expenses and some payments had to be eliminated. He simply couldn't afford it anymore. The policy may have just run out; or, the term simply expired before Joe did.

The following are the main two reasons that companies don't pay the death benefit for a term life insurance policy:
1. The policy simply expires because it is a term policy and the term expires before the insured person dies.
2. The insured person stops making the payments for whatever reason.

So, how many term life insurance policies actually pay a death benefit? That means "what do you think the odds are that you will die while you are covered by the policy? 75%? 50%? 25%? 10%?" The answer is: it's a very, very small number. Many in the industry say it is less than 5%. The consensus seems to be 2 to 3%. A few say even less than 1%. Whatever the real number is, it's one of the main reasons that life insurance is such a bargain. The life insurance companies simply don't have to pay the death benefit.

Why is that, exactly? Well, let's look at the two main reasons. Remember, we're talking about term policies. Term policies are purchased for a specific term and for a specific reason. Not dying when the policy is in force, or the insured simply stops paying the premium, are the two main reasons that term life insurance is such a bargain.

As an example, a forty year old father buys a twenty year term policy because in twenty years the kids will be out of college and the house will be paid for. Specific term and specific reason. The probability of his dying within that term is slim because his life expectancy is at least another twenty years after the term expires when he is 60.

The other reason is plain old economics. The policy simply lapses before the term is up. Policies lapse every day because the insured no longer has the money to make the premium payment, or he simply chooses to stop paying for whatever reason.

Summarizing, the death benefit is not paid for the majority of people who own traditional term life insurance because the term is too short. The coverage is there when they are least likely to die. The term is often made even shorter because they stop making the payments and the policy lapses.

Remember, people tend to buy traditional term life insurance when they are younger and there is a possibility they might die. They should also be buying it when they are older when there is a probability they might die.

Once again, your probability of being stricken with any critical, chronic, or terminal illness is greater than dying at any age.

Chapter 11

Why don't more people have life insurance?

Well, the answer to that very valid question is this. Some people really don't need it. If they were to die and no one would suffer financially because of their death, why do they need life insurance? Since it's paid after the fact of dying, is there really any need? Nope. No need. No life insurance.

What about the ones who don't have life insurance but actually do have a need. That need is someone who would suffer financially if they were to die, such as a spouse, the children, or someone else they might be supporting such as parents or a child from a divorce. It could also be for business partners or an employer that considers them indispensable. Lastly, it could be for any debts that could occur and estate taxes that might need to be paid.

Let's talk about those people who don't have life insurance but actually should have it. What is their thinking? Why don't they have it? Here are some common reasons.

1. They think they don't need it.
When they're young, most don't think about it because the odds are so low that they would die. Even when they start a family, buy a house, or have other responsibilities that might impact someone financially if they were to die, they still keep it low on their priority list, if it's even there at all. It's the "out of sight, out of mind" mentality.

2. They think they can't afford it.
Even with the television and radio ads touting low cost life insurance, many think that they might have to spend upwards of $50 to $100 a month or more just for basic life insurance, not knowing how inexpensive term life insurance actually is. As an example, a healthy 40 year old, non-

smoker, male or female, could buy a $100,000 ten year traditional term life insurance policy for less than $13.00 per month.

3. They don't understand it.
They think it's hard to qualify. They don't understand the process. They don't want any kind of medical exam. It's just too much trouble.

4. They don't know who to talk to.
They're not comfortable dealing with life insurance salesmen or companies.

5. They see no current benefit.
Many people aren't interested in anything that doesn't provide an immediate benefit. Traditional life insurance doesn't provide any benefit at all as long as the insured person is alive. It seems that some people don't like the idea that they wouldn't personally benefit from having life insurance coverage.

6. They have a fear of their own death.
They don't want to talk about it much less anticipate it or any ramifications thereof. It's a macabre topic and, therefore, taboo.

7. They don't believe they are going to die.
At least not for a very long time. It's not that they fear death. They just can't imagine its happening to them. This could be demonstrated by the way they think and talk about it, in thoughts and sayings like: "I'm not old enough to die. I'm in great health. Why would I die? I have too many things left to do. It's just not my time. My family has a history of longevity. I have a long time to go before I die."

8. They think they just don't need it.
No reason. They just don't want it and they don't want to talk about it.

There are many rationalizations as to why people think they don't need life insurance. When you think about the fact that less than 5% of all term life insurance polices are actually paid, it lends a certain validation to their thinking, no matter how misguided it may seem. Actually, a traditional term life insurance policy would pay 50%, more or less of the time, if it were just owned til age 80.

The new way to own life insurance, "life insurance you don't have to die to collect" increases the percentage of collecting the death benefit to over 80%, without dying, when owned to age 80. It takes the perspective of owning life insurance to a new level and reason. Not only will someone have over an 80% chance of collecting the death benefit, they currently have about a 70% chance of collecting it by the time they reach 65 – and that's without dying. Remarkably, the average age of being stricken with a critical illness is 43. Fortunately, most who are stricken recover and many go on to live long lives.

The folks who really have a valid reason for not needing life insurance now actually have a valid reason to own "life insurance you don't have to die to collect." That's because they are the one who could suffer financially if they were stricken with a life threatening illness.

Chapter 12

How are life insurance premiums determined?

Premiums are the payments made to an insurance company to pay for the policy. There are three ways to own a life insurance policy and the premiums are determined accordingly.

1. *Guaranteed issue life insurance* requires no medical exam and is the most expensive type of insurance to own. Guaranteed issue is a term used to describe a situation where a policy is offered to any eligible applicant with little or no regard to health status. The premiums are solely determined by the applicant's age, sex, and amount of the death benefit, It is the simplest, albeit the most expensive, way to own life insurance. Typically, because of the added health risks and other unknowns, the death benefit will only be paid after the policy has been in force for two years. If the insured dies before two years have elapsed, the death benefit will not be paid. Instead, the total premiums paid to that point will be refunded to the beneficiary, usually plus interest.

2. *Simplified issue life insurance* requires no medical exam and is neither the cheapest nor most expensive way to go. It is less costly than guaranteed issue but more costly than fully underwritten life insurance. Simplified issue means you answer a few questions about your medical history for the life insurance application rather than undergoing a medical exam. The insurance company will usually also do a medical background check. Not everyone who applies for simplified issue will be approved. Depending on the answers to the questions on the application and the medical background check, the applicant can be declined or accepted for either a standard or substandard approval. The premiums are determined by these answers and the background check.

If there are health issues, the policy may not pay the death benefit until after it's been in force for two years. If there are serious health issues, the applicant may have to own guaranteed issue life insurance. Otherwise, the death benefit can be paid as soon as the policy is approved and the first payment is made. The premiums are determined by the applicant's age, sex, whether he's a smoker or non-smoker, amount of the death benefit and his health condition, as determined by routine questions and the medical background check.

3. Fully underwritten issue life insurance means that a medical exam is required. This will give you the lowest rates and highest death benefits. Unless you are highly averse to medical exams, such as a fear of needles, it is almost always best to own life insurance that has been fully underwritten.

A medical exam can consist of numerous tests. The presence of any health issues, the applicant's age, whether he's a smoker or non-smoker, and the amount of the death benefit, all influence the number, and the nature, of the tests.

Besides the premiums being determined by age, sex, and amount of the death benefit, there are other specific factors that are considered. They are as follows:

1. Current Health.
This is the basic consideration. Do you have any health issues such as high blood pressure or high cholesterol? Are you on any medications? Are you overweight? Are you a smoker? Have you had any health issues in the past? If you can answer no to all of these questions, you are probably in really good health and can qualify for the best rates.

2. Age.
Your age is one of the primary factors that determines your life insurance premiums. Since the policy will pay when you die, the insurance company wants to know what your life

expectancy is. The longer you are expected to live, the greater number of premiums you will pay. The older you are when you buy your policy, the higher the premium will be because of the likelihood of your death happening sooner rather than later. Simply put, the younger you are, the less your premium should be.

3. Smoker or non-smoker.
Smoking is a huge negative when it comes to life insurance premiums. Because smoking is known to cause cancer and other health problems, premiums can increase 3 to 5 times compared to a non-smoker. The older you are, the greater the disparity. Chewing tobacco can also increase the premium compared to a non-smoker. Some studies say that smokers will live an average of 10 years less than a non-smoker.

4. Height and weight.
Life insurance premiums are also based on your height/weight proportion. All life insurance companies have charts that adjust the premiums depending on your height/weight proportion. You may be healthy, but if you are overweight, your premiums could be higher, the amount depending on the degree your height-to-weight ratio varies from the ideal range.

5. Profession.
Some occupations are more dangerous than others and contribute to determining premiums. An office manager typically is considered a safer occupation than a police officer or fire fighter where the risk of being killed on the job is higher. The more risk your job presents, the higher the premium may be. Some examples of riskier jobs that could cause higher premiums are: pilot, certain construction workers, and sky diving instructors just to name a few.

6. Medical History – yours and your family's history.
As mentioned, your current health is a basic determiner of your premium. Your family's history can also impact your

premium. If one or both of your parents died at a relatively young age due to health issues, your premium could be higher. If a particular illness runs in your family such as cancer or heart disease, that also could make for higher premiums.

Your medical history – including any current health conditions – can all have an impact on your premiums. But, you could have been stricken 5 or 10 years ago with cancer or something equally serious and fully recovered with no serious after effects. You're in good health now. You may qualify for better or even the best rates because of your current health and the time that has elapsed. Health conditions may result in higher premiums, but only those that have the potential to reduce your lifespan.

It is important to note here that you should never think that you may not be eligible for life insurance because of current or past health problems. It costs nothing to apply for life insurance and there is no cost to you for the physical exam you may be required to take. If you are declined by one company, or quoted a high premium, simply apply to another. Not all approval processes are created equally.

When applying for life insurance, unless you are applying for guaranteed issue or simplified issue, the insurance company will require a physical examination. They will rely on your answers provided on the medical questionnaire, so it's important to be as honest and accurate as possible. Depending on your current health, your age, and the amount of life insurance you are applying for, you may not be required to have an extensive medical exam. It may be as easy as a simple blood test and urine specimen. Sometimes companies will just request a report from the Medical Information Bureau, or MIB. This report can provide a history of doctor visits, surgeries, hospital stays, and known health conditions. Between your information given on the questionnaire, the results of your physical, if needed, and the MIB report, they'll have a pretty good assessment of your medical history. Just like your credit bureau report indicates your credit history, the medical bureau report indicates your medical history.

If you haven't seen a doctor in a while or do not have a primary care physician, this may delay the approval of the policy. There may not be any MIB information available or it may be too old to be relevant. Sometimes an applicant is healthy, hasn't seen a doctor in years because they haven't had a reason, and doesn't even have a primary care doctor. That in itself doesn't mean you won't qualify. It just means it may take longer to determine your actual health status. Remember, there is no cost to you for the physical exam. The insurance company covers that cost.

7. Other factors can affect your premium.
Factors such as hobbies, foreign travel, your credit, and your driving record may also be considered. Hazardous activities, such as different kinds of racing, hang-gliding, and scuba diving, to name a few, may all increase the risk of death. Traveling to certain foreign countries may also be considered to be dangerous and an increased risk of death. If you have had recent, multiple, traffic violations such as speeding tickets or a DUI, your premium may increase. Any activities outside the norm may also increase your premium because of an increased risk of death.

8. Gender.
Life expectancy for women is greater than for men so they will typically pay less for life insurance premiums for a policy with the same death benefit and same age as a man.

9. The actual policy death benefit.
As mentioned, the amount of the death benefit also determines how much you will pay. Very simply, the larger the amount of the death benefit, the higher the premium.

Finally, after review, the life insurance company assigns you a classification. Your life insurance health class is determined by the results of these specific factors mentioned. It is important because the higher the class rating, the lower the cost of your insurance premium.

The various class categories are generally defined as follows:

- Preferred Plus non-smoker: This is considered the best category for a life insurance health rating. People in this category have an excellent health history. They are not taking any medications, and they are within the guidelines for height and weight. They are healthy and have no family history of diseases. Only about 5% of people qualify for this class.

- Preferred non-smoker: This is considered the second best category in life insurance health classes. You are deemed to be in excellent health with a few minor health issues that may or may not be treated with medication, such as high cholesterol. You are within the guidelines for height and weight. You may have a family history of cancer or other diseases. You may also participate in dangerous activities such as risky sports or risky work occupations.

- Standard Plus non-smoker: You are considered to be in better than average health, but you may have minor health issues. You may be slightly over the height and weight guide, but you also have no family history of diseases. There are different variables that could put you in this category.

- Standard non-smoker: Although this may be in the bottom of the four general life insurance health classes, it is considered to be one of the most common categories. You are of average health and take multiple medications. Your height and weight guidelines may not meet the requirements, and you may have a family history of cancer or other diseases.

- Preferred Smoker: Same general guidelines as preferred, but applicant is a smoker. Depending on the insurance company, if he has been a non-smoker for an acceptable period of time, usually 12 to 60 months, he may be considered a non- smoker. Some companies offer non-smoker rates instead of smoker's rates if the applicant is only using chewing tobacco or cigars.

- Standard Smoker: Same general guidelines as standard non-smoker, but with the current use of tobacco products. Some companies offer non-smoker rates instead of smoker's rates if the applicant is only using chewing tobacco or cigars.

What happens if the applicant doesn't fit into one of the six categories listed?

Not all applicants may qualify for one of these categories and yet they could still be eligible for coverage. Their health issues or lifestyles may prevent them from fitting into one of the regular classifications. But, they can still be rated in accordance with their coverage risks. Life insurers call this further classification system a table rating system. Instead of preferred or standard categories, an applicant might be given a table rating, with a number or letter to designate their rating, such as table 1, 2, or 3 or table A, B, or C.

Depending on that rating, the applicant will pay an additional percentage of the regular premium if approved for a life insurance policy. Table ratings can be given for medical or non-medical reasons. Some examples could include high blood pressure, previous cancer, diabetes, or your combined height and weight, especially obesity. Other reasons could be a history of mental illness or your occupation. An applicant who might qualify for a standard rating but has a history of multiple convictions for driving under the influence or someone who pilots small planes would also be examples of someone who could receive a table rating.

Table rating simply refers to the increased life insurance premiums charged to people who cannot qualify for regular rates because of an increased risk of dying. Anything that increases the likelihood of premature death may trigger a table rating. Whether you are a smoker or non-smoker, once you don't qualify for their standard rating, you enter the area of substandard, or table rating. Substandard simply means below average life expectancy and high risk life insurance.

Again, some reasons for these ratings may be: height/weight considered obese; treatment for chronic illnesses or major health conditions (such as recent/prior heart attack, cancer, diabetes); abnormal lab results, just to name a few.

These are typical substandard ratings. They are expressed as a table rating and are usually designated as Tables A-J or Tables 1-10. Each additional table increase is typically a 25% increase over the standard risk class rates, or as follows:
Table A rating: Standard rate + 25%
Table B rating: Standard rate + 50%
Table C rating: Standard rate + 75%
Table D rating: Standard rate + 100%
Table E rating: Standard rate + 125%
Table F rating: Standard rate + 150%
Table G rating: Standard rate + 175%
Table H rating: Standard rate + 200%

Table I rating: Standard rate + 225%
Table J rating: Standard rate + 250%

Note: these figures for substandard ratings are general examples. Not all life insurance companies' ratings are the same and can vary with each company.

If you are turned down for life insurance by one company, you may still qualify for coverage from another. The key is to work with a non-captive agent, or one who has access to more than one, or several, companies. A captive agent is one who can only represent one insurance company.

Also, health is not the only determining factor. Table ratings can be assigned for other reasons like a criminal background or history of DUIs. Again, investigate all of your options when seeking coverage. Just because one company turns you down, or rates you, doesn't mean that they're the only one who could insure you. Other companies may be happy to insure you even if at an increased premium rate.

Chapter 13

Reasons you may be declined or rated.

Here are a few reasons why you could be turned down for life Insurance, or be rated as sub-standard and face higher premiums, and what you can do.

A Personal History of any critical or serious illness.
A history of a major illness such as cancer doesn't necessarily mean you will be declined, especially if it's been at least two years and you are in good health now. If you have recovered from a serious illness, the longer it's been since you were originally stricken, the more likely you will be approved. It's not unusual to also qualify for good rates. If you are currently being treated for a major illness, it's unlikely that you will be approved.

Deceased Parents.
If your parents died young as a result of poor health, the insurance companies take this into consideration when approving you. If one, or both, of your parents were stricken with a major illness at an early age, usually before 65, you're at a higher risk of suffering the same fate. This, in itself, shouldn't be cause for being declined, but you may be uprated to a higher premium.

Obesity.
The insurance companies use a rating table based on your height and weight. Studies show that over a third of the adults in America are overweight. Obesity is officially defined as a body fat of 32% or more for women and 25% or more for men. While life insurance companies may accept applicants on the lower end of the scale, extreme obesity is typically grounds for denial. This is due to the fact that obesity links closely to conditions such as diabetes and heart disease.

High Blood Pressure.
The CDC reports that one in three American adults has high blood pressure. High blood pressure is closely linked to heart attacks, strokes, and chronic heart failure. Less than half of all people who suffer from high blood pressure have their blood pressure under control. Nearly a third of American adults have prehypertension which can lead to high blood pressure. Getting screened for prehypertension and taking action to lower your blood pressure early are two of the best ways to avoid developing this condition.

High Cholesterol.
Approximately one in six Americans suffers from high cholesterol. You can check your levels with a simple blood test. This condition is often preventable with a healthy diet and regular exercise. While high cholesterol won't typically be a decline, your rates for life insurance will likely be higher if your cholesterol levels aren't well controlled. On the other hand, high cholesterol combined with other health conditions could result in a decline.

Recent Hospitalization.
Applicants who were recently hospitalized are more likely to get declined for life insurance than those who've stayed healthy and injury-free. If you've just gotten out of the hospital for a health issue like a heart attack or stroke, an insurance company may want to wait 6 months or longer to see if you've made a full recovery before approving you.

Pre-existing Health Problems.
Heart disease, diabetes, epilepsy, and many other pre-existing conditions will either result in an increased rate or a decline. The end result will be based on treatment, how long you have had the condition, and how well controlled it is. Since some conditions, like type 2 diabetes, are often preventable, it's important to think ahead about how your health choices today can impact your future. Get screened for pre-diabetes and other health conditions regularly if you're at risk, and talk to your doctor about ways to stay well.

Tobacco and/or Alcohol Use.
Tobacco and/or excessive alcohol use create big negatives on your life insurance application. Alcohol has both immediate and long-term risks. In the short-term, you can suffer from alcohol poisoning, injury, and risky behaviors while you're intoxicated. Long-term alcohol use leads to neurological, psychiatric, and cardiovascular problems as well as many liver diseases. The effects of smoking cause one in five deaths in America and can lead to cancer and heart disease.

Drug Use.
Your life insurance company will want to know about any kind of drug use, both legal and illegal. Illegal drug use is an obvious reason for denial. Unfortunately, the regular use of legal medications may harm your case as well, as this is typically a sign of an underlying medical condition that requires regular treatment. While most illegal drug use will cause a decline, many life insurance companies will approve you for marijuana use – although you may pay higher rates for coverage.

Dangerous Hobbies.
If you spend your weekends rock climbing or skydiving, life insurance companies are more hesitant to cover you. If accepted, you'll likely pay more for coverage. While you may find these activities a fun way to keep active and stay fit, your insurance provider will see the potential for serious injury or death. A few dangerous activities that your life insurance company will likely frown upon include scuba diving, hot air ballooning, bungee jumping, aviation, and racing, just to name a few. How often you participate in these activities will be a factor in determining whether or not you pay a higher rate – for example scuba diving just once or twice a year will typically not cause a higher rate for coverage.

Foreign Travel.
Travel outside the country on a frequent basis to countries considered high risk may result in a decline for life insurance coverage. Exotic travel comes with potential risks including disease and injury. Life insurance companies classify countries as A, B, C, or D destinations. Travel to A level countries carries minimal risk while visiting D countries is more dangerous. You need to report any plans for future travel on your insurance application, both for pleasure and for work.

Traffic Violations.
Safe drivers not only get the best auto insurance rates, they also have a better chance at getting good life insurance premiums. If your driving record is full of traffic violations and accidents, your insurance provider will immediately see the high potential for more accidents in the future. If you have several moving violations within the past five years, you will likely not qualify for the best rates. A DUI will lead to higher rates as well, and more than 2 DUIs in the past 10 years could result in a decline.

Dishonest Application Information.
Your application will ask if you've applied for life insurance before and if you've ever been declined. If you have, it's crucial that you fess up and admit it since the insurance company can determine if you have recently applied for coverage. Be honest about all other questions on your application as well. Don't guess on measurable questions such as your height and weight. You'll most likely have to submit to a physical examination anyway.

There are many reasons that an applicant may be uprated to a higher premium or declined. If this happens to you, don't give up. Your agent can have the insurance company take a second look. Occasionally, pertinent information was overlooked or improperly interpreted. If that doesn't work, apply to another company. Remember, there is no cost to apply. Any medical exams are paid for by the insurance company.

The important thing to remember here is that usually, when it's harder to get life insurance, it's because you are a higher risk and therefore, have a greater need. Just because you may not be able to get the coverage you want, or the premium you want to pay, doesn't mean you shouldn't take what you are offered and can afford.

Don't be stubborn. If you are uprated, it means you have a higher probability of suffering a life threatening illness and actually dying.

Chapter 14

Common life insurance mistakes.

There is much more to owning life insurance than just deciding on how much to buy and whether to buy term or permanent life insurance. Here are some important, but, lesser known, examples of things to consider.

You named your estate as beneficiary.
Naming your estate as beneficiary of your life insurance means the proceeds may be subject to needless state inheritance taxes or to a higher rate than if the proceeds were payable to a named beneficiary. This mistake also makes it certain that creditors have full access to the life insurance proceeds even though most states' laws provide full or significant exemption from the claims of creditors for life insurance payable to named beneficiaries such as a spouse, children, parent or sibling. By naming your estate as your beneficiary, you guarantee that the precious dollars you wanted to go to a loved one will be subjected to the expense and potential aggravation and delay of probate. This can also be alleviated by having a trust instead of a will. Consult with an estate planning attorney. Usually the first consultation is free. Don't hesitate to ask questions.

You only named one beneficiary.
If your only beneficiary dies before you do, and you haven't named any other beneficiaries, the proceeds will be paid to your estate. You should have at least one contingent and one tertiary beneficiary. You should also review your policy every few years or so to make sure you don't want, or have, to change the beneficiaries. Also, it's a good idea to review coverage after major life events, such as marriage, divorce, remarriage, and having a baby.

All the insurance on your life is owned by you.

If you're in a high income bracket and if your estate is likely to be large enough to be exposed to federal estate taxes, owning insurance in your own name may lead to needless federal estate tax inclusion. That is something to avoid if you have such an estate. For 2017, the estate and gift tax exemption is $5.49 million per individual, up from $5.45 million in 2016. That means an individual can leave $5.49 million to heirs and pay no federal estate or gift tax. If your estate is worth more than this exemption amount, the life insurance proceeds could be included as part of the taxable estate. To solve the problem, you can have a trust purchase and own the policy, or you can give the money for premiums to an adult beneficiary to own and pay for the policy. You can give up to $14,000 per year to any individual free of federal taxes. If you never own the policy or have any rights in it, under present tax law, it can't be included in your estate, even if you give your adult child or trustee cash gifts that are then used to pay premiums. If your estate is sizable and you have a financial adviser, accountant, and estate attorney, all whose advice you respect, all of you should sit down with your insurance agent. All of you should be involved in the discussions and subsequent decisions. You may have a top notch financial adviser, top notch attorney, top notch accountant, and top notch insurance agent, but, separately they may be only experts in their own field.

The Goodman Triangle or "the unholy trinity."
Life insurance has always been known for providing tax free proceeds to the beneficiary. Typically, the death benefit is paid tax free… except when it's not tax free. How can this happen? There's one particular situation where gift taxes can apply and be substantial. Remember, there are three parties to a life insurance policy. The first party, the insured, is the person on whose life the policy benefits are based. The second party, the policy owner, is the person that controls the policy and has all rights of ownership of the policy. In addition, the owner is responsible for the premiums. The third party, the beneficiary, is the person who receives the proceeds, the death benefit, at the death of the

insured. The beneficiary has no other rights to the policy. Certain combinations of life insurance policy ownership and beneficiary designations can lead to severe gift tax situations. This tax situation can be avoided by ensuring the ownership and beneficiary designations of the life insurance policy are properly structured.

Very few people, including life insurance agents, are aware that, if the owner of a life insurance policy is not the insured, and the owner names a third party as beneficiary, then the owner is considered to have made a taxable gift of the death benefit to the beneficiary at the death of the insured. This is what happened in the famous court case, Goodman v. Commissioner of the Internal Revenue Service. Violations of this so called Goodman Triangle can occur frequently among family members. Typically, one spouse will own the policy insuring the life of the other spouse and name a child as beneficiary. The result of this arrangement is this. Upon the death of the insured spouse, the owner spouse is considered to have made a taxable gift of the full death benefit to the child. Any amount over and above the $14,000 per person per year gift tax annual exclusion would be considered a taxable gift and begin reducing the owner spouse's lifetime gift exemption. Using the lifetime gift exemption for this purpose reduces the amount the spouse can pass estate tax free at his or her death to other family members. After exhausting both the annual exclusion and lifetime exemption, any remaining death benefit would be subject to current gift tax rates. To avoid a violation of the Goodman Rule, the policy should be structured so that either the insured and owner are the same person, or the owner and beneficiary are the same person. While some of these combinations may still result in estate, gift or generation skipping transfer tax — proper planning may be able to lessen the amounts subject to taxation. It is critical to consult with and rely on your independent legal and tax advisers regarding your particular set of facts and circumstances.

Simply put, there are three parties in a life insurance policy, but there should only be two people involved. If there are three people involved, it violates the Goodman Rule and makes the owner subject to a tax liability, not the beneficiary who actually receives the death benefit. Again, for more specific details, consult an insurance adviser, tax adviser and/or an estate attorney – or just only have two people involved in the policy.

Naming a minor as a beneficiary.
You own a life insurance policy for your children's benefit. However, naming them as beneficiaries on the policy when they're still minors is typically a bad idea. If you die before they've reached legal adulthood, the life insurance company cannot pay benefits to minor children until the court appoints a guardian. That can take time and money for attorney fees and court costs. Better to name your spouse or other trusted adult as the beneficiary. You could also set up a life insurance trust for the children and name the trust and trustee as the beneficiary on your life insurance policy. You can stipulate how the money should be used. An estate attorney should advise you.

Keeping your life insurance policy a secret.
Some people don't like to talk about their personal finances, especially life insurance. But someone needs to know so the beneficiary can make a claim. Besides a spouse or adult children, other people who should be aware of your policy are your accountant, your estate planning attorney, and anyone you appoint in your will or trust. They should also be aware of the location of the policy, such as a safe. There's no reason not to give them a copy of the cover sheet showing the insurance company contact information and the policy number.

There are many mistakes, errors of commission and errors of omission, that we all may make regarding life insurance. Don't get frustrated and let worry keep you from owning life insurance. Sometimes the worst decision is the one we don't make. Own a policy today.

Chapter 15

Why would a life insurance company not pay the death benefit?

Approximately 99% of all death benefits are paid. That's the good news. The bad news… well, there really isn't any bad news. The other 1% of death benefits not paid are usually the fault, or misfortune, of the insured. Here are some reasons why life insurance companies don't pay the other 1%.

Life insurance policies typically come with a provision referred to as a period of contestability. The life insurance contestability period is a time frame in which insurance companies can investigate and deny claims. This period is two years in most states and one year in others. The clock starts ticking the date the policy goes into effect. If you die within the contestability period, the life insurance company can investigate whether you were honest on your life insurance application. The company can deny paying the death benefit if you lied -- even if the cause of death has nothing to do with lying on your application. Lying is an example of material misrepresentation. Let's say that when you filled out the application, you indicated you are a non-smoker. What you neglected to disclose is that you do occasionally smoke. If you die within the two year contestability period and the life insurance company discovers that you lied on the application, they may decline paying the death benefit. If you smoke pot, you must disclose that on the application. Smoking pot in itself will not cause most companies to deny issuing you a policy. In fact, many companies don't consider it to be that big of a deal. They may rate you, but not as much as if you actually smoked cigarettes The biggest problem here is if you lie on the application, it gives the company the ability to contest the claim and possibly not pay it. Companies don't necessarily scrutinize every policy when the death occurs within that two year window. They will typically pay the death benefit when it occurs within the contestability period. They just have the right to take a peek to see if there were any improprieties. As an aside, if you are late with your premium and your policy lapses, you may be able to get the policy reinstated. Most insurances companies want to retain your business. If this happens, typically, you will have a new period of contestability starting from the time your policy was reinstated. A new period of contestability can also start if you transfer your existing policy to a new policy. Just remember – reinstatement or new policy equals a new period of contestability. Something you should keep in mind.

Here are a few reasons that life insurance companies can refuse to pay the death benefit.

Suicide.
Life insurance companies will not pay the death benefit if the insured commits suicide within the suicide clause period as defined in the policy. If someone takes their own life, unless it's beyond the suicide clause, the death benefit will usually not be paid. Typically, the life insurance company will only refund the premiums paid. Everyone needs to be aware of the suicide clause.

Homicide.
So long as the insured is not involved in an illegal activity when murdered, the death benefit should be paid. If the beneficiary is the murderer, the death benefit will probably not be paid. It would go to the contingent beneficiary or the insured's estate.

Illegal activities.
This falls under the common sense category. If you die while committing a crime, or are participating in any kind of illegal activity, the life insurance company can refuse to pay the death benefit.

Dangerous activities not disclosed.
Life insurance is all about risk. For example, if you are involved in jumping out of perfectly good airplanes with a parachute, you are a higher risk applicant than someone who only flies commercially. You can still jump, but your premium may be increased. If you are an occasional, recreational jumper, you may pay less than your sky diving instructor. Jump less. Pay less. So be sure to disclose your dangerous hobbies or lifestyle when asked. If you are actively, even occasionally, involved in one of the dangerous activities listed on the application, you can still do it, but you might have to pay for that protection.

Claiming you are a non-smoker when you actually are a smoker.
Whether you smoke a pack a month, a pack a day, or you only light up occasionally, you are still considered a smoker. Just because you might think you don't smoke enough to consider yourself a smoker, the insurance company considers it their decision to make. If you were a smoker and quit, indicate when you quit. If it were 2 years ago, indicate 2 years ago. If it were 6 months ago or 10 years ago, tell the truth. If you under report your smoking status, the insurance company now has reason to challenge paying your death benefit. Same advice goes if you smoke, or smoked, cigars, a pipe, used snuff, chew tobacco, or even smoked pot – and yes, brownies may count. Remember, honesty is the best policy.

Not disclosing health issues.
This is another common sense category. If you have any health issues, either current or in the past, disclose them. You might think you got a great premium because the insurance company missed something about your health, but it could give them cause to not pay the death benefit if they find out after your death.

Living outside the United States.

When you initially purchase a policy, there are questions about traveling, and living, outside the United States. These are important questions to answer carefully and truthfully. Traveling outside the United States usually isn't an issue but living outside the United States can be, even if it's part time. Restricted countries are just that. Restricted. If you die in a restricted country, the death benefit probably won't be paid. It's the same if you are killed in "an act of war." The important thing to do here is to discuss it with your agent and specifically disclose the circumstances. Again, honesty is the best policy.

Fraud.

Once again, when it comes to life insurance, honesty is always the best policy. The insurance company may investigate the cause of your death. They will look at the circumstances that led to your death and then look at your original application. If they discover that you had certain health conditions, or that you were involved in dangerous activities all the way back to the time of your original application and you didn't disclose them, the company can deny paying the death benefit.

Discrepancies between a life insurance policy and a will.

I included this example to show how there can be confusion between a will and a life insurance policy. A designation in a will or trust cannot override a designation of an earlier beneficiary in a policy unless the policy in question is named in the will or trust. For example, if you get divorced and remarry, but your ex-wife's name is on the insurance policy as your beneficiary, then the policy will be paid to your ex-wife even if the will, or trust, designates the second wife as the beneficiary. The named beneficiary on the policy receives the death benefit. The solution is simple. Change the beneficiary on the life insurance policy to your current wife's name or whomever you choose to be the current beneficiary. You should review your insurance every year or so.

Your policy lapsed.
There are only two reasons why a policy lapses, or ends. First, the premiums don't get paid. Sometimes policies lapse because the premium is automatically taken from a checking account. If the account is subsequently closed and the life insurance company is not notified that the premium has to come out of another account, guess what? The premiums are not being paid and the policy will lapse.

Next, term policies are just that. They last for a specific term. Sometimes people don't realize their policy has lapsed because the term is up. They may not be aware it expired because the premiums were automatically deducted from their checking account and they're just not paying attention. The term ends and they have no life insurance. Term policy holders should always know the date their term ends. The life insurance companies will send notices that the policy is about to expire to prompt the insured to get a new policy. There have been instances where the policy holder thought the notices were junk mail and simply threw them away. Pay attention when your insurance company mails you anything. Make sure you know when your tern policy expires and apply for a new policy at least two months before the old one expires so there is no lapse in coverage.

When applying for life insurance, don't hesitate to ask questions – about anything - regarding the application. Remember, the only dumb question is the one you don't ask.

Chapter 16

How important is a life insurance company's rating?

All life insurance companies are financially rated. Financial strength ratings consider the probability that a life insurance company will be able to pay its financial obligations, most importantly, its claims. There are four main rating agencies, A.M. Best, Fitch, Moody's, and Standard & Poor's. Each rating agency evaluates insurers slightly differently, but ratings are generally based on factors such as a company's financial holdings, and how much it's collecting in premiums compared with how much it's paying out in claims. As a general rule of thumb, any life insurance company with a rating of at least a B is considered financially strong.

The important thing to know here is that all the best known life insurance companies are financially strong.

Chapter 17

Causes of death.

Statistics are an important part of everyday life. They influence weather forecasts, medical studies, political campaigns, sports, and the stock market, just to name a few examples.

We all know we are going to die. That's a 100% certainty. But, what else can statistics tell us? They can tell us what the probabilities are as to how long we will live. That's our life expectancy. How about how we're going to die? Will it be by natural causes? By an accident? Homicide or suicide? Will it be a sudden death or a prolonged illness? There's a statistical probability for just about anything you can think of.

Let's consider life expectancy. A report issued by the National Center for Health Statistics in December, 2016 indicates that a male baby born today has a life expectancy of 76.3 years and a female baby born today has a life expectancy of 81.2 years. Furthermore, a 65 year old male today has a life expectancy of 18.0 more years, or age 83.0, and a 65 year old female today has a life expectancy of 20.6 more years, or age 85.6. Besides telling us that women tend to live longer than men, it also tells us that the longer we live, the longer we can expect to live.

Consider there are only 4 ways to die.

1. *Natural causes (you get sick*.).
   These account for over 92% of all deaths.
2. *Accidents (includes any kind).*
   They are the #1 cause of death up to age 45. It ranks 4th in all causes of death.
3. *Suicide.*
   It ranks 10th in causes of death.

4. Homicide.
It ranks in the high teens in the top 20 causes of death.

As indicated, death by natural causes account for over 92% of all deaths. When people kill themselves, are killed by someone else, or are killed as a result of any kind of accident, it's considered non-natural causes and accounts for almost 8% of all deaths.

Next, let's look at how likely we are to die by natural causes. The top ten causes of our demise are:

1. Heart disease.
Heart disease is the leading cause of death for both men and women in the U.S. It is also the leading cause of death worldwide. Men account for more than half of the deaths that occur as a result of heart disease.

2. Cancer.
Cancer can strike anyone. Most types of cancer risk increase with age. Higher or lower risk is due to differences in exposure to carcinogens such as from smoking or occupational related risks. Risk can also be a result of genetic factors. Lung cancer is the number one cancer killer in both men and women.

3. Chronic lower respiratory diseases.
Chronic Lower Respiratory Disease (CLRD) was called Chronic Obstructive Pulmonary Disease (COPD) until 1999. CLRD is made up of three major diseases; chronic bronchitis, emphysema, and asthma. All three diseases are characterized by shortness of breath due to airway obstruction. This obstruction is irreversible in chronic bronchitis and emphysema. It is reversible in asthma. Smoking is a primary risk factor of CLRD. Approximately 80 percent of CLRD deaths can be attributed to smoking.

4. Accidents (unintentional injuries).

Accidents, including any and all kind, are the 4th leading cause of death in the U.S. They are also the leading cause of death for those aged 1-44.

5. Stroke (cerebrovascular diseases).
Stroke is a disease that affects the arteries leading to and within the brain. Not only is it the number 5 cause of death, it is a leading cause of disability in the U.S. The first symptom of a stroke is a stroke. That means there is only a small window of opportunity to get the victim to a doctor or to an emergency room. If you suspect that someone might be having a stroke, there are four simple actions you can take to determine if it might be a stroke.
1. Ask them to smile. Does one side of the face droop?
2. Ask them to talk and speak a simple sentence. Is their speech slurred or strange?
3. Ask them to raise both arms. Does one arm drift downward?
4. Ask them to stick out their tongue. Is their tongue crooked or go to one side or the other?
If you answer yes to any of these questions, immediately call 911 even if the person resists. You are the best person to determine whether or not to call 911. If you are not sure, call 911 anyway. Better to be safe than sorry. Time is of the essence. Doctors say that if a stroke victim can be treated within the first three hours, they have a good chance for survival and lessened disability. As with any medical emergency, if you have to think about calling 911, stop thinking and just call. Better to be safe than sorry.

6. Alzheimer's disease.
It is usually not the direct cause of a person's death, Death occurs from complications from Alzheimer's. Most people with Alzheimer's are 65 and older. However, over 200,000 Americans under the age of 65 have early onset Alzheimer's. Increasing age is the greatest known risk factor. Deaths from Alzheimer's disease may be underestimated, because death certificates often list pneumonia or another complication as the cause of death, rather than the

underlying Alzheimer's disease. Future studies may indicate that when Alzheimer's is more accurately disclosed on death certificates, the actual deaths attributed to Alzheimer's may increase dramatically.

7. Diabetes.

Diabetes is all about controlling your blood sugar levels. A person with Type 1 diabetes (and some with type 2) need to take insulin to process glucose. The glucose cannot be processed if these people do not take insulin. This can lead to hyperglycemia, or high blood sugar. Hyperglycemia is an abnormally high blood glucose (blood sugar) level. It is considered a tell tale sign of diabetes (both type 1 diabetes and type 2 diabetes) and prediabetes. The danger with hyperglycemia is that it can lead to ketoacidosis, diabetic coma and, ultimately, death if left untreated. First symptoms can be excessive thirst, fatigue, blurry vision, frequent urination and an upset stomach. Ketoacidosis symptoms can be shortness of breath, fruity smelling breath, nausea, vomiting, and dry mouth. Can you die from diabetes? Yes, but with normal insulin intake, proper blood sugar monitoring and healthy living you could live a normal or near normal life. People with type 2 diabetes carry a 15 percent increased risk of premature death compared to healthy people.

8. Influenza and pneumonia.

Influenza is a highly infectious respiratory disease. It is caused by certain strains of the influenza virus. When the virus is inhaled, it attacks cells in the upper respiratory tract, causing typical flu symptoms such as fatigue, fever and chills, a hacking cough, and body aches. Influenza victims are also susceptible to potentially life-threatening secondary infections.

Pneumonia is a serious infection or inflammation of the lungs. The lung's air sacs fill with pus and other liquid, blocking oxygen from reaching the bloodstream. If there is too little oxygen in the blood, the body's cells cannot work properly, which can lead to death.

9. Nephritis, nephrotic syndrome, and nephrosis.
These are diseases associated with the kidney. Kidney disease is most often caused by diabetes or high blood pressure.

10. Suicide - Intentional self-harm.
Suicide is the act of intentionally causing one's own death. It is the second leading cause of death of those age 10 to 34. It's the fourth leading cause of death of those age 35 to 54. By age 65, it has dropped out of the top ten causes of death only because there are so many age related illness deaths. Suicide among the elderly is a dramatically high number.

9. Nephritis, nephrotic syndrome, and nephrosis. These are diseases associated with the kidney. Kidney disease is most often caused by diabetes or high blood pressure.

10. Suicide - Intentional self-harm. Suicide is the act of intentionally causing one's own death. It is the second leading cause of death of those age 10 to 34. It's the fourth leading cause of death for those age 35 to 54. By age 65, it has dropped out of the top ten causes of death only [illegible] suicide among the elderly is a [illegible] number.

Chapter 18

Why you should own term life insurance to at least age 80.

We know that less than 5% of traditional term policies are ever paid. While some policies simply lapse because the insured just stops making the payments, most polices expire because the scheduled term ends. This happens most often when the insured is not close to his life expectancy age when the term ends and doesn't die. The real issue here is that more term policies would pay if the term were longer, at least until age 80, the current average life expectancy.

It's very simple. The older we get, the closer we are to dying. Term life insurance is inexpensive, but the consumer doesn't seem to be aware of the value. For example, a 50 year old non-smoker, in good health, might pay about $42 per month for $100,000 coverage for a thirty year traditional term life insurance policy to age 80. He has about a 50% chance of dying before age 80 and having his beneficiary receive the $100,000. But, he has over an 80% chance of suffering a qualifying medical crisis before age 80, and if he owns "life insurance you don't have to die to collect," then he can collect the death benefit before dying... and don't forget, 70% Of everybody who reaches the age of 65 will have been stricken with either cancer, a heart attack or stroke – and survived. If he lives to age 80 without dying or suffering a life threatening illness, he receives no cash benefit. He simply paid for the protection and peace of mind. His total cost would have been $42 X 360 (30 years premium) = $15,120. Or he could have owned "life insurance you don't have to collect" to age 80 and increased his probability of collecting the death benefit to 80% without dying. That probability increases to 90% if the term coverage is increased to age 90.

Chapter 19

Some questions and answers.

1. I already have a traditional term life insurance policy and I have a supplemental cancer policy that also provides coverage for heart attack and stroke. How does this new, updated term life insurance compare?
"Life insurance you don't have to die to collect" contains coverage for the same critical illnesses that your supplemental policy has. But, it also includes up to 14 additional defined critical illnesses, plus it provides chronic illness coverage and terminal illness coverage. Typically, your supplemental policy's rates adjust every five years – that means they increase and the maximum amount of the benefit they can collect is much less than the available coverage here. If you total the amount of premium you're paying for your traditional term life insurance and the amount of premium you're paying for your separate supplemental policy, you'll find that the single premium you would pay for "life insurance you don't have to die to collect" should be substantially lower. Also, it will never increase during the term. Your supplemental policy typically increases every five years. Remember, the maximum "living benefits" coverage is available up to $2,000,000.

2. I have a great medical plan at work and it includes life insurance. Why would I want to consider this?
Employer medical plans are always great to have and they are getting rarer. Consider this to be just inexpensive supplemental coverage. Here are some questions about potential benefits: does your current medical plan cover experimental treatment? What would you do If you were to lose your benefits? What if your health changed and you became uninsurable? What if you had to provide your own hospitalization plan? How about being offered a great job opportunity but the health plan wasn't as good? There are

lots of reasons to have this, even if it's a small policy amount. You can get a lot of benefits for under $50 month.

3. I'm a smoker but I'm planning on quitting. I know the premium will be higher. Why shouldn't I wait until I quit and then apply?
Yes, the premium will be higher. But you have to have stopped for at least a year or more before your premiums might be less. All that time you would have no coverage. The best thing to consider is to apply for a policy now, pay the higher smoker's rate, and then you would be covered until you could apply for reduced, non-smoker rates. When the time has passed that you would qualify for a non-smoker rate, apply again and get a new policy. You should be able to pay the higher premium for being considered a smoker with the savings you'll have from quitting. Remember, the financial cost of smoking is not as serious as the medical cost of smoking. There is no valid reason to wait.

4. I lost my existig policy. How can I get copy?
Call the insurance company and request a copy. They can find your policy information with your name, address, social security number and your birth date. If you're not sure who the insurance company is, look at your billing statement that you receive. If your insurance premium is automatically deducted from your bank account, look on your monthly bank statement. The information will be there. Call your bank if necessary.

5. My company pays for a life insurance policy on me and receives the death benefit if I die. Will this new policy allow them to collect the death benefit if I am eligible because of a medical crisis?
Yes, if they are the owner and the beneficiary. This is called key man coverage or key person coverage. As the owner and beneficiary, they are entitled to any benefit paid.

6. How does the premium cost for this new, "life insurance I don't have to die to collect," compare to the premium cost for

traditional term life insurance that I see advertised on television, radio, and the internet?
It is very similar and sometimes costs less than traditional, outdated term life insurance, such as you see on the media. All traditional term life insurance companies can charge whatever they choose to charge and some are simply more expensive.

7. I have current health issues and have had difficulty getting insured in the past. Can I be covered with this updated life insurance?
Maybe. It is typically no more difficult to qualify for this updated term life insurance than it is for the outdated traditional term life insurance. The underwriting is typically the same. Many applicants can get approved because the health issues occurred years ago. More current health issues may require a higher premium, but you may still be approved. If you're being rated and charged a higher premium that means you're a higher risk. That also means that your probability of collecting the death benefit before you die, especially before age 80, is much greater. The important thing to remember is, there is no cost to apply. Any medical testing required to qualify you is paid by the insurance company. There is no valid reason to wait.

8. I like "life insurance you don't have to die to collect" and want to apply. My insurance is ending in six months. Why shouldn't I wait until then?
Much can happen in the next six months. You could suffer a medical crisis. Any change in your health history can affect the premium. A simple trip to the emergency room can trigger a higher premium. A current health screening can also disclose an unknown health change. There is no valid reason to wait.

9. I'm well off financially. Why would I need this?
Wealthy people sometimes need cash that is more readily available when there is any kind of financial crisis. That's what this is designed to do; make cash available when you

have a cash flow problem - a financial crisis caused by a medical crisis. Let's consider that you're not sick. Tomorrow, if you could have $100,000, or $500,000, or even $1,000,000, would you have a use for it? An extra $100,000, or $500,000, or even $1,000,000 seldom hurts anybody, especially at the time of a medical and a financial crisis.

10. I had health issues in the past. Can I get this new, updated coverage?
Many past health issues can have little to no effect on qualifying for a new policy. It depends on the time elapsed and your current health. It costs nothing to apply. You may also get an update on your current health.

11. Everyone in my family has lived to be older than 90 and seldom were sick. Why should I consider this?
That is not unusual. But, studies show that many senior citizens older than 80 and 90 have also had children who died much younger. While great genes are a plus, there are always exceptions.

12. No one depends on me for financial support. No one will suffer when I die. Why should I consider this?
"Life insurance you don't have to die to collect," is primarily for one beneficiary, you! If no one will suffer financially when you die, the real question is, "will you suffer financially when you get sick and suffer a medical crisis? When you experience a medical crisis, do you think an extra $100,000, or more, might come in handy? Remember, it's tax free and you can spend it anyway you see fit.

13. I want to replace my existing policy with a new policy. How do I do that and what should I know?
First of all, NEVER cancel an existing policy until you have a replacement policy in place. You have to be sure you can qualify for a new policy. You need to submit a new application for whatever you want to buy, and when the new policy is issued, then and only then, should you cancel the

old policy. Here's how to cancel a policy. While insurance premiums can be paid quarterly, semi-annually or annually they are typically paid monthly. If it is a term policy that you are paying monthly and you stop paying, it should automatically cancel after 30 days. You still should notify the life insurance company that you are canceling. If the premium is automatically deducted from a bank account, you must also cancel that. No matter how you are paying, there are generally no refunds. If it is a cash accumulation policy such as whole life and you stop making payments, the accumulated cash value could continue making the payment until the cash value reaches zero. If you do have accumulated cash value, you can cancel the policy and receive that cash value. You must notify the company if you want to cancel and the accumulated cash value will be given to you. In either event, if you plan on replacing your policy, do not cancel it until the new policy is in place. You want to be sure you can qualify for another policy and the new policy is in effect before cancelling your old policy

Always remember: NEVER CANCEL AN EXISTING POLICY UNTIL YOU HAVE A REPLACEMENT POLICY IN PLACE!

Chapter 20

Another perspective.
Why I should I own this until I'm 80.

I was a little apprehensive about writing this chapter because I thought it might be a little macabre. Then I realized this topic is actually somewhere between macabre and reality. I then decided that since we're all going to die, why not make the most of it - the dying part anyway. In other words, carpe mortem.

Thirty per cent of seniors, 55 years and older, have little or no savings. By the time we all reach the age of 80, there are only three scenarios: we're sick, we're dead, or we're healthy and we're going to keep on living. If you own "life insurance you don't have to die to collect," two out of three of the scenarios will result in your death benefit – or living benefit - being paid, most likely to you before you die. Remember, very few people die healthy.

Let's consider some possibilities.

Jack, a 50 year old healthy male, non-smoker, can own a "life insurance you don't have to die to collect" policy, to age 80, with a $100,000 death benefit for about $42 per month. If he is stricken with a defined critical, or chronic, illness, he can collect the death benefit without dying because he's his own beneficiary. Let's say at age 70 he's stricken with cancer. He collects 75%, or $75,000, of the death benefit based on the severity of the illness – remember, the amount he can collect is based on how life threatening the illness is. It doesn't have to be a terminal illness. Generally, the benefit amount is between 65% and 85% of the death benefit. He paid $42 a month for 20 years, or a total of $10,080, for a net return of $64,920, which, by the way, is tax free. If he were stricken with a terminal illness, one that gives him 12 to 24 months to live as determined by the policy, he can still collect a percentage of the death benefit. Should he live to age 80 and he's healthy, it would have cost him $15,120 ($42 X 360 months or 30 years) for the coverage. The term is now up, the premiums end, and there no longer is a death benefit.

Changing the death benefit for Jack to $500,000 means his premium would now be about $141.00 per month. If he is stricken at age 70, he would have paid $141.00 per month for 20 years. That totals $33,840. Let's say he could collect 75% of $500,000 or $375.000. His net return would be $341,160. If he reaches age 80 and is healthy, he would have spent $50,760 ($141 X 360 months or 30 years) for the coverage. Again, the term has ended and there are no longer any benefits available

What happens if he's exceptionally healthy? He doesn't get sick. He doesn't die. He turns 80. His life insurance just expired, He paid $50,760 over thirty years for $500,000 worth of benefits that he had over an 80% chance of collecting. He beat those odds by not getting sick or dying. The question here might be, should he be upset?

Remember, if you're going to spend money on term life insurance, why not take advantage of the opportunity to actually be able to collect your death benefit before you die. Owning "life insurance you don't have to die to collect" and paying premiums to an older age is not gambling when you'll suffer a medical crisis or when you'll die. You're simply confronting the inevitable.

… just a little food for thought.

Chapter 21

Some statistics and other random offerings.

There is much to be gleaned from statistics.
We have learned about one of life's sure bets – that we're all going to die. That's a 100% certainty.

- By the time we turn 65, 70% of us will have been stricken with a heart attack, cancer or stroke. Most will survive. Many will die from an additional critical illness, not the first.
- We can suffer a life threatening critical or chronic illness, recover and still live much longer. We can actually suffer 2 or more such illnesses, recover, and live a long life.
- The average age of the first incident of one of these three illnesses is 43.
- If we have a traditional term life insurance policy, we have less than a 5% chance of collecting the death benefit because the term will expire before we die (we outlive the term), or we simply stop paying the premium. In other words, it expires before we do.
- Every year over 25 million Americans survive a first incident of heart disease, cancer, or stroke.
- Over 15.8 million Americans suffer a heart attack every year. 70% survive.
- Over 60% of all cancer patients live at least 5 years after the first incident.
- Nearly three-quarters of all strokes occur in people over the age of 65.
- More than 80% of strokes are preventable by changing, treating, or controlling risk factors.
- Alzheimer's is the sixth leading cause of death.
- Over 5,000,000 Americans have Alzheimer's.

- One in nine people age 65 and older have or will contract Alzheimer's disease.
- Over 60% of all bankruptcies are medical bankruptcies.
- Almost 80% of those medical bankruptcies occurred even though the consumer had medical insurance.
- 1 out of 2 men and 1 out of 3 women will be stricken with cancer.
- 100% of all Americans are going to die. But, If they own "life insurance you don't have to die to collect," at least until they are age 80, they have over an 80% probability of collecting the death benefit without dying.
- Average life expectancy has increased a lot, but maximum life span has increased little if at all.
- Your probability of being stricken with any critical or chronic illness is greater than dying at any age.
- More than 92% of all deaths are due to natural causes. That means someone gets sick first.
- Traditional term life insurance only pays when we die. "Life insurance you don't have to die to collect" pays when we are stricken with a life threatening illness and don't die. The cost is similar.
- Nobody buys life insurance hoping they will collect on it. They buy it for peace of mind, as a safeguard in case something dire happens.
- Now it is beneficial to own life insurance for the living benefits and be able to collect the death benefit without dying.
- No part of living benefits is any kind of long term care or any kind of disability coverage.
- The best part about owning traditional life insurance is you have less than a 5% probability of collecting the death benefit.
- Once you understand how "life insurance you don't have to die to collect" works, when you are stricken with a medical crisis, this insurance will be the first thing you think about whether you own it or not.

- Owning life insurance and paying premiums is not gambling when you'll die. You're simply confronting the inevitable. If you're going to spend money on premiums, why not take advantage of the opportunity to actually be able to collect your death benefit when you may need it the most - before you die. Owning "life insurance you don't have to die to collect" affords that opportunity.
- In many instances, it's more important to own "life insurance you don't have to die to collect" for the living benefits rather than the death benefit

Chapter 22

What is final expense insurance?

Final expense life insurance is also known as burial insurance. It's marketed mostly to lower income seniors, with little or no assets, and who are age 60 and over. It's designed to provide money to cover final expenses such as funeral costs, final medical bills, and any miscellaneous remaining debt such as credit cards. It's very expensive compared to what could otherwise be purchased before age 60. It typically is a whole life policy that accumulates some cash value. But, most are designed so that the insured will be paying premiums at least until age 100. The premiums are high compared to the actual death benefit. A 60 year old male, non-smoker, in good health would pay about $75 a month for $18,000 coverage or death benefit. The reality is that same 60 year old would pay about $73 per month for $50,000 coverage to age 80 for "life insurance you don't have to die to collect" that would include critical, chronic, and terminal illness coverage. This coverage would let him collect the death benefit when he suffered a medical crisis and didn't die. I understand this isn't an apples to apples comparison, but it is food for thought. Had he bought $100,000 coverage at age 55, for a twenty five year term until age 80, his monthly premium would only be about $70 per month.

The downside: if he owns "life insurance you don't have to die to collect" to age 80 and doesn't die, or isn't stricken with something that the living benefits will cover, he no longer has any coverage. But, it's something to think about.

Chapter 23

Closing.......

"There's nothing more powerful than
an idea whose time has come."

One of my favorite quotes, by Victor Hugo.

"Life insurance you don't have to die to collect" is a great example of an idea whose time has come. It's already changing lives. Many of us have heard stories from folks - friends, neighbors, relatives, co-workers, acquaintances, clients – about people who were stricken and survived a critical or chronic illness. Some of these folks will admit that they frequently thought it would be better for them to die so their family could collect their death benefit. It would stave off the ensuing financial disaster. Some who recover from the medical crisis never recover from the resulting financial crisis, no matter what their age.

What is frustrating to me is this: I frequently talk to people who already have traditional term life insurance and are paying a monthly premium. After learning about "life insurance you don't have to die to collect," they understand that, except in extremely rare instances, they will get sick and suffer a medical crisis before they die; they understand that they have less than a 5% probability of having their death benefit paid by their traditional term life insurance policy; they understand that they can have over an 80% to 90% chance of collecting their own death benefit with "life insurance you don't have to die to collect" - before they die; they understand that the cost of this new updated term life insurance is comparable to – and sometimes is less – than the premium they are already paying for their outdated traditional term life insurance. After all this understanding, they still choose to ignore all the benefits of "life insurance you don't have to die to collect." I think to myself, "you're already paying for something that's gold plated. Why wouldn't you pay a similar price for something that's solid gold?"

Here are some typical responses:
"I get all my insurance from one agent. I'll talk to him."
(Agents who sell multiple lines of insurance such as homeowner's insurance, auto insurance, and life insurance, are typically captive agents, meaning they can only offer one company's products - and their company doesn't offer this.)

"I only do business with my brother-in-law."
(It's always nice to keep business in the family, but if your brother-in-law knew about and sold this product, you would already own it.)

"I'm okay. I'm happy with what I have."
(I have no idea why the understanding or motivation is not there.)

While I have a passion for this product, I understand that not everyone thinks like me. That all being said, if you fully understand how "life insurance you don't have to die to collect" works, it will be the first thing you think about when you suffer a medical crisis. My only hope is that, when that happens, you will, in fact, own "life insurance you don't have to die to collect."

Chapter 24

How can I get more information about "life insurance you don't have to die to collect?"

First of all, I want to again point out that this new, updated term life insurance, "life insurance you don't have to die to collect," is comparable in premium cost to the outdated traditional term life insurance that you may already be paying for. What does that really mean? In many cases, it's no new money out of your pocket if you update your existing insurance. Sometimes it's even less. There are many life insurance companies that charge more for their traditional outdated term life insurance.

As mentioned, there are only a handful of life insurance companies that offer this new, updated term life insurance product. It is not advertised and only marketed through each company's agents. While the product with each company is similar, each company offers it with its own unique guidelines. No one company is best suited for all applicants. Each company has its own little niche.

If you already have an insurance agent, consult with him or her first. Although most agents are not familiar with the few companies that do market this product, many are anxious to learn more once they understand the additional benefits and the comparable cost.

Whether you're a consumer or an agent, for more information, please visit the website:

outdatedlifeinsurance.com

BONUS

I would like to know what you think of "Is Your Life Insurance Outdated?" As a thank you for contacting the website and reviewing the book, requesting more information, asking a question, or simply leaving a comment, I would personally like to offer you a free copy of my next book tentatively titled "Is Your Tax Free Retirement Plan Outdated?" Details are on the website. This is a limited time offer and may be withdrawn at any time.

outdatedlifeinsurance.com

You can also contact me with any questions or comments at:

georgestewart1@yahoo.com

Thank you, George L. Stewart

Notes

Notes